This book belongs to:

_____

African Safari Counting Book

Our Legaci Press, LLC

African Safari Counting Book: Learning Numbers 1-20
Text copyright © 2018 Jessica Ann Mitchell Aiwuyor
Written and designed by Jessica Ann Mitchell Aiwuyor

Images on pages 4-24 © Graphics Factory.com
African continent image courtesy of iStockphoto © Oleg Chepurin
Additional images courtesy of BNPDesignStudio, Clairev, Seamartini, Fusion Books, Twemoji, Djvstock2, Djvstock, Studiog, and Studiog2 via Canva licensing.

This book or any portion thereof
may not be reproduced or used in any manner whatsoever without the express written permission of the publisher except for the use of brief quotations in a book review.

Printed in the United States of America.

First Printing, 2018

ISBN 978-1-948061-06-3

Our Legaci Press, LLC
P.O. Box 471221
6514 Marlboro Pike
District Heights, MD 20747

www.OurLegaciPress.com

Hi, I'm Alex.

I like to have fun and learn with my friends.

Let's go on an African safari together.

A safari is an adventure to see wild animals.

Africa is big and full of amazing animals.
We will learn our numbers
by counting them.

1

One wild ostrich.

The South African Ostrich has long legs with black and white feathers.

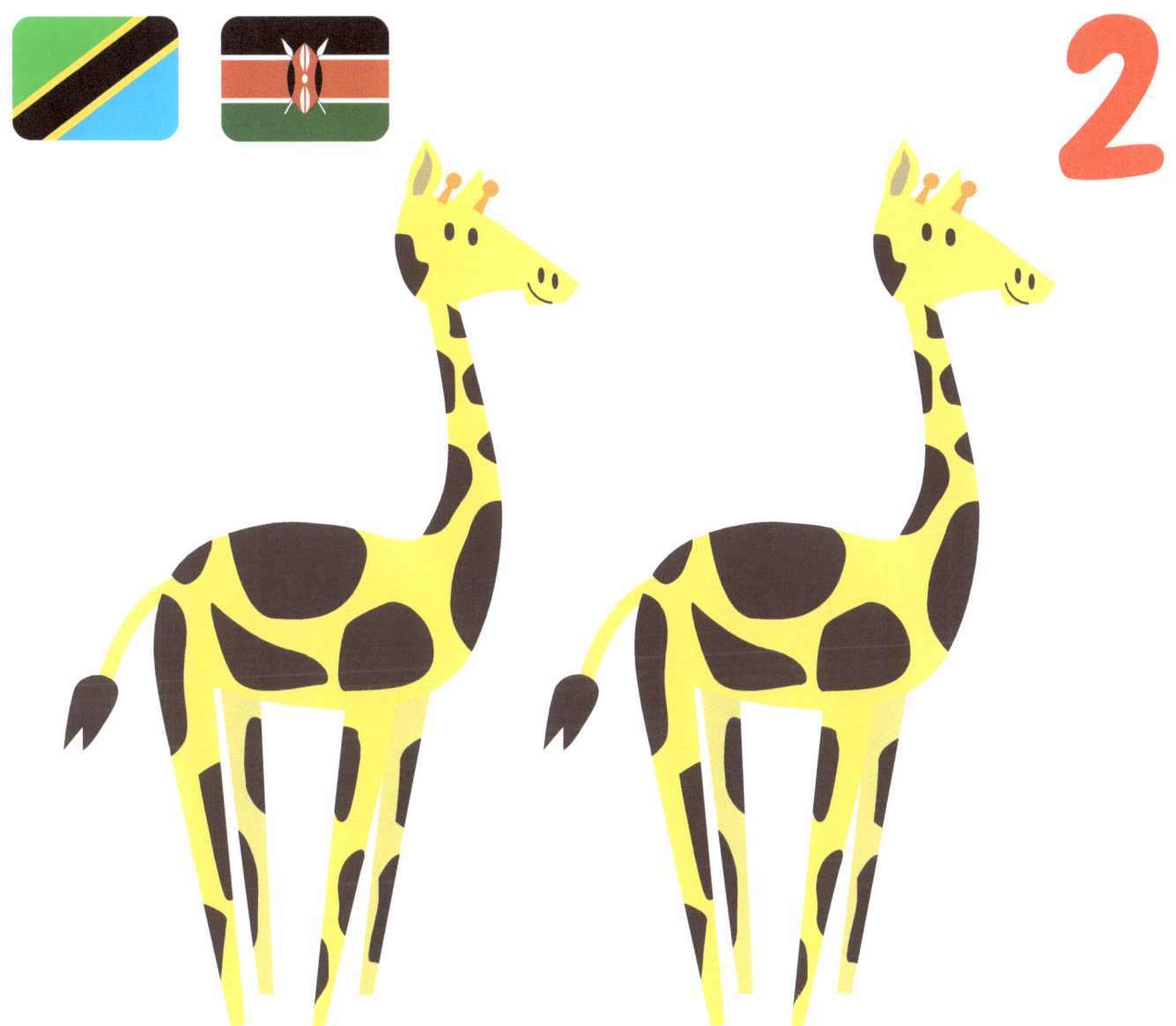

Two long-necked giraffes.

Masai Giraffes live in Tanzania and Kenya.
They have long necks and brown spots.

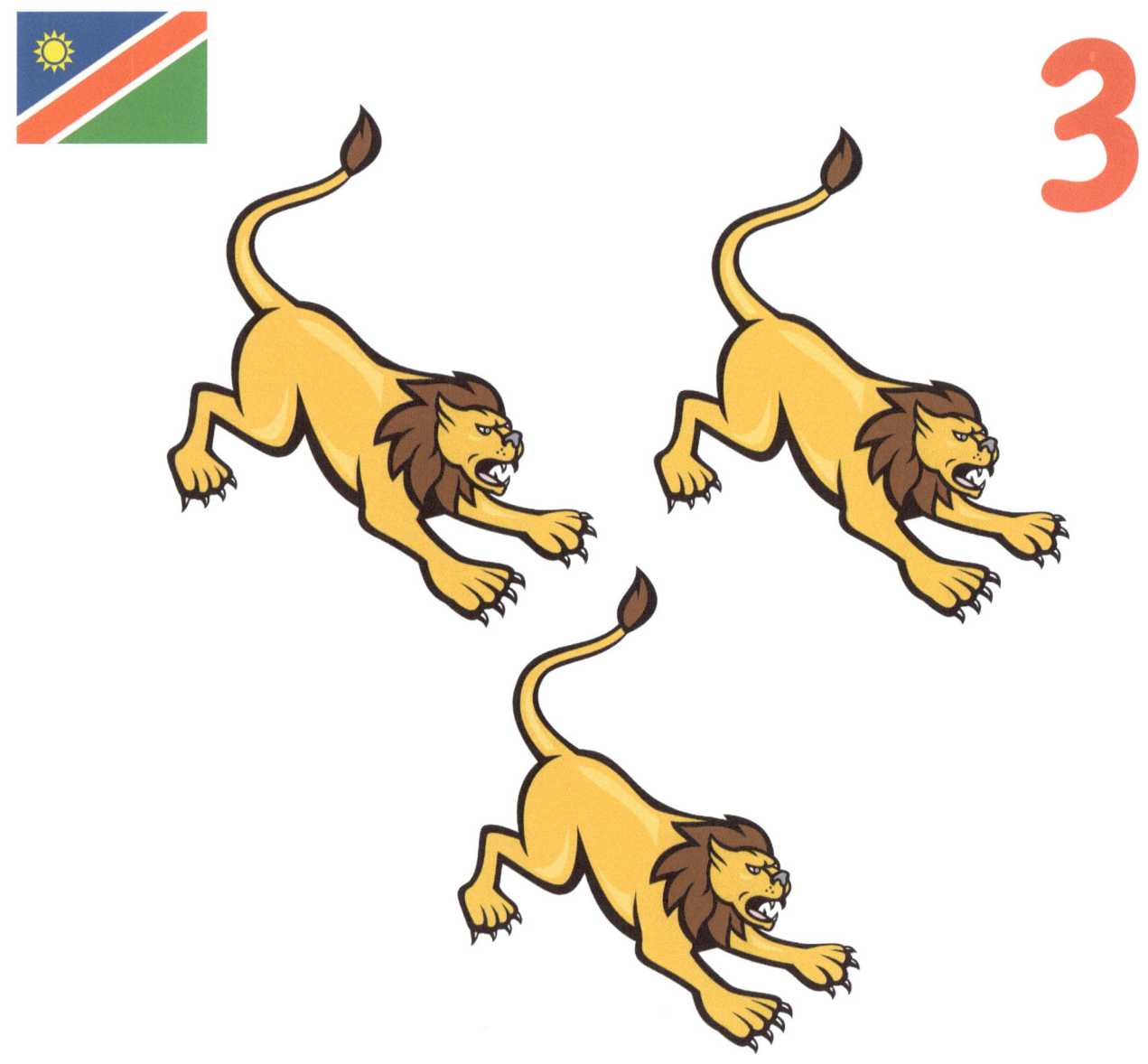

Three roaring lions.

Lions are golden brown with a big mane of hair.
They make a loud roaring sound. Many live in Namibia.

Four gray elephants.

Elephants are large and gray with ivory tusks.
They are smart. Many live in Botswana and Zimbabwe.

Five horned rhinoceroses.

Rhinos are gray colored with thick skin and two horns. Many live in Angola and Mozambique.

Six slithering snakes.

There are many kinds of snakes in Africa. Gaboon Vipers are black, brown, and yellow. Some live in Guinea-Bissau.

7

Seven striped zebras.

Zebras are related to horses. They have black and white stripes. Many live in Uganda.

Eight spotted cheetahs.

Cheetahs have spots. They can run really fast.
Some live in South Sudan and Ethiopia.

Nine galloping antelope.

Antelope like to run and jump. They have two horns and brown fur. Many live in Namibia.

Ten talking parrots.

Parrots have different colors. Some can talk like humans. Many live in Madagascar.

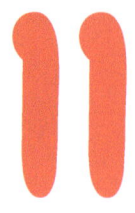

Eleven laughing hyenas.

Hyenas have spots or stripes with sharp teeth.
They make a laughing sound. Many live in Rwanda and Benin.

12

Twelve grazing buffalo.

African buffalo love to eat grass. They are brown and big, with thick skin. Many live in Burkina Faso.

13

Thirteen gray hippopotamuses.

Hippos are good swimmers. They can even sleep in water.
Many live in Cameroon.

Fourteen humpbacked camels.

Camels have large backs with one or two humps.
Many live in Somalia and Egypt.

Fifteen trekking tortoises.

Tortoises live in their thick shells. They love to eat grass. Many live in Mauritania and Chad.

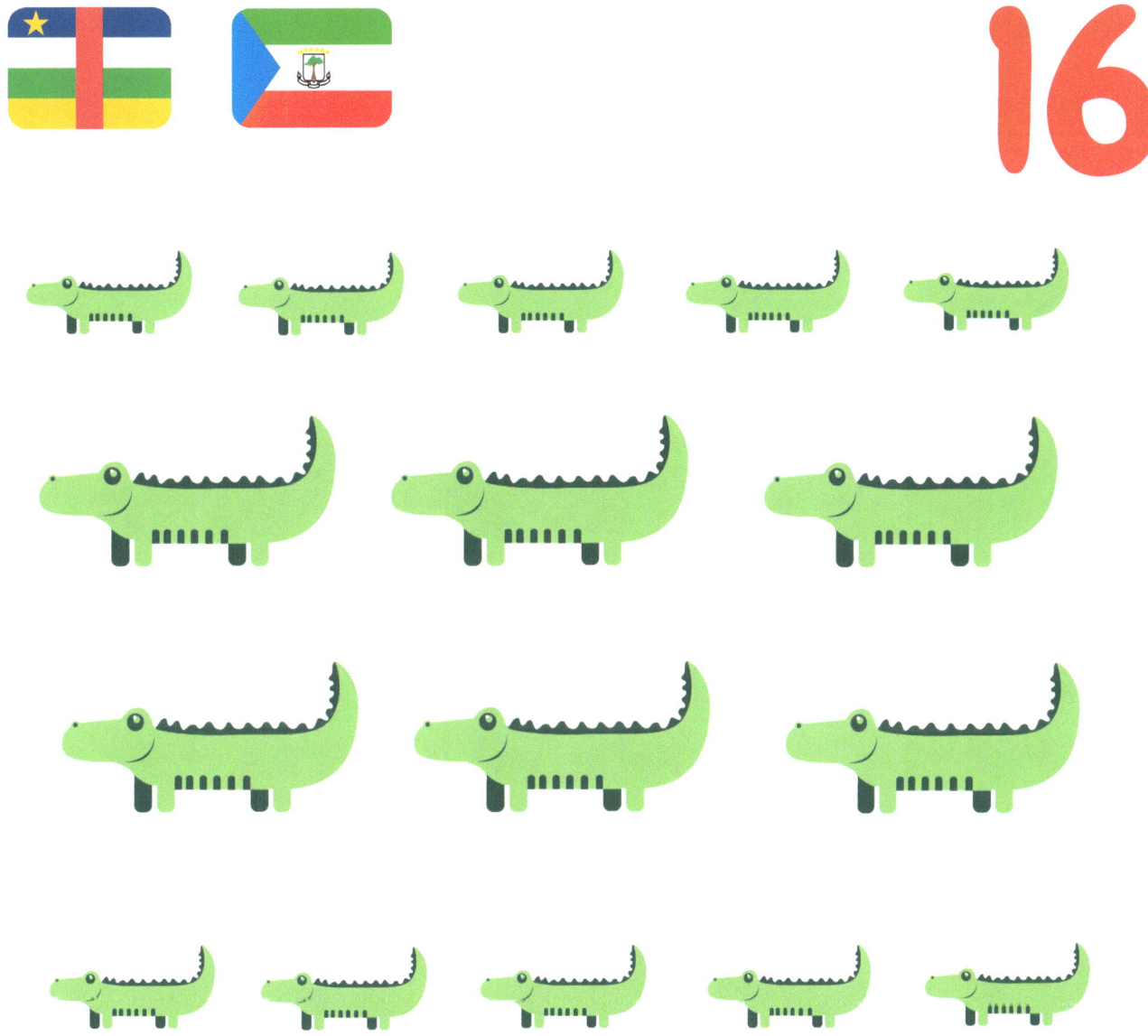

Sixteen snapping crocodiles.

Crocodiles live in lakes and rivers. They have sharp teeth. Many live in the Central African Republic and Equatorial Guinea.

Seventeen green bullfrogs.

African Giant Bullfrogs are big and green. They make loud croaking sounds. Many live in Swaziland and Malawi.

Eighteen colorful fish.

There are many types of fish in Africa.
One type of fish is called Chilotilapia. They live in Malawi.

Nineteen buzzing bees.

African Honey Bees are black and yellow.
They make a buzzing sound. Many live in Ghana.

Twenty dancing monkeys.

Monkeys like to play games. They sit up high in trees.
Golden monkeys live in the Democratic Republic of Congo.

Wow, there are so many cool animals in Africa! Thank you for going on a safari with me. Learning with you is fun.

Now, it's time to count:

1, 2, 3, 4, 5,

6, 7, 8, 9, 10,

11, 12, 13, 14, 15,

16, 17, 18, 19,

20.

Great job!

www.ingramcontent.com/pod-product-compliance
Lightning Source LLC
Chambersburg PA
CBHW050749110526
44591CB00002B/22